ANDREW JACKSON

A Photo-Illustrated Biography
by Steve Potts

Bridgestone Books
an Imprint of Capstone Press

JB
Jackson

Facts about Andrew Jackson

• Andrew Jackson was the seventh president of the United States.

• He was born in a log cabin.

• He fought in the Revolutionary War and the War of 1812.

• His nickname was Old Hickory.

Bridgestone Books are published by Capstone Press • 818 North Willow Street, Mankato, Minnesota 56001
Copyright © 1996 by Capstone Press • All rights reserved • Printed in the United States of America

Library of Congress Cataloging-in-Publication Data
Potts, Steve, 1956-
    Andrew Jackson, a photo-illustrated biography/ by Steve Potts.
    p. cm.--(Read and discover photo-illustrated biographies)
    Includes bibliographical references and index.
    Summary: A brief biography of the seventh president of the United States.
    ISBN 1-56065-455-4
    1. Jackson, Andrew, 1767-1845--Juvenile literature. 2. Presidents--United States--Biography--
Juvenile literature. [1. Jackson, Andrew, 1767-1845. 2. Presidents.]   I. Title. II. Series.
E382.P8 1996
973.5'6'092--dc20
[B]

                96-25857
                CIP
                AC

Photo credits
Archive Photos, cover, 4, 12, 14, 16.
Corbis-Bettmann, 6, 10.
Florida Department of Commerce, Tourism Division, 8.
FPG, 18, 20.

Table of Contents

Words in **boldface** type in the text are defined in the Words to Know section in the back of this book.

The Boy from Carolina

Andrew Jackson is remembered as one of the greatest American presidents. During his life, many exciting things happened to the young United States. The country won its independence from England. It expanded west to the Mississippi River and south to Florida.

And it saw a young boy from a log cabin grow up to be president. America owes Andrew Jackson for much of its success.

Andrew was born on March 15, 1767, in an area called the Waxhaws. This area was on the border between North and South Carolina. His family had moved there from Northern Ireland. Andrew was named after his father, who had died three weeks before he was born. Andrew moved with his mother to a relative's house.

There Andrew was surrounded by a large, loving family. He had two older brothers and eight cousins. Andrew liked to play tricks on his family. He was almost always in trouble.

Many exciting things happened to the country during Andrew Jackson's life.

The Revolutionary War

Andrew did not like school, especially spelling. He probably had the least education of all the presidents. But he loved to read. And he was good at it.

Andrew was nine years old when the American **colonies** declared their independence from England in 1776. Andrew read the new Declaration of Independence in the town square for those who could not read. The American colonists were very unhappy with their British rulers. They wanted to be independent. They fought for their freedom from 1776 to 1781.

The Revolutionary War hurt many American families. Andrew and his brothers served in the army. Both of his brothers died. Andrew's mother died as well. Andrew did not escape the war either. He was taken prisoner. When a British officer ordered him to shine his boots, Andrew refused. The officer hit him across the face with his sword. For the rest of his life, Andrew hated the British for what they had done to his family.

A picture by Currier & Ives shows Andrew Jackson defying a British officer during the Revolutionary War.

Young Lawyer

The Revolutionary War ended in 1781. A peace treaty was signed two years later. The Americans won the war and their independence from England. After the war, Andrew's uncle in Ireland died and left him $1,500. In the 1700s, most people would have used that money to buy land. Andrew did not. He thought he could gamble and make even more money. He gambled all his money on horse races. He lost. His money was gone.

Andrew decided to earn a living as a lawyer. He studied law for three years. He became a lawyer in 1787.

There were not many jobs for lawyers in the Carolinas. Andrew moved west across the mountains to Nashville. It was in the territory that became the state of Tennessee. Andrew liked studying law. People came to watch when he argued in the courtroom.

Andrew Jackson became a lawyer in 1787.

Rachel and the Hermitage

In 1791, Andrew married Rachel Donelson Robards. She had been married to a man who abused her. Two years after their marriage, Andrew and Rachel made a shocking discovery. Rachel had not been legally divorced from her first husband until 1793. They were horrified to learn that Rachel had been married to two men at the same time. Andrew and Rachel remarried in 1794.

Many people gossiped about Andrew and Rachel. This angered Andrew. He was always willing to settle disputes by **dueling.** Andrew fought two duels and was wounded twice. Andrew's temper was strong.

Next to his wife, Andrew loved the Hermitage more than anything. It was a large plantation outside Nashville. Andrew bought it in 1804. Like many people in the South, Andrew owned slaves. He did not believe slavery was wrong. He treated his slaves well. Andrew and Rachel adopted a boy from Rachel's family. The Hermitage was an active, busy place.

Andrew wore a similar picture of Rachel Jackson around his neck on a chain after she died.

Old Hickory

War came to the United States again in 1812, when America fought the British. Andrew was a general in the Tennessee **militia**. The War of 1812 made him a hero. And he got a nickname, too. A soldier said Andrew was tough as a hickory branch. His nickname became Old Hickory.

In 1814 Andrew was ordered to go to New Orleans to defend it against the British. Although the British had a strong army, it was no match for Andrew's men. His army of frontier settlers, Indians, freed slaves, and pirates killed hundreds of British soldiers.

Andrew then fought the Seminole War in Florida. He and his men killed Seminole chiefs and burned their homes. But the Seminole Indians refused to surrender.

Spain owned Florida but agreed to sell it to the United States. Andrew served as governor of Florida for a short time in 1821. Later, most of the Seminole were forced out of Florida. But some survived and their **descendants** still live in Florida.

Andrew Jackson got his nickname, Old Hickory, during the War of 1812.

Running for President

Andrew had served in the House and Senate in the late 1790s. He wanted to return to Washington, D.C. This time he wanted to go there as president.

He almost won the 1824 election. He was the choice of the voters. Because of election rules, the House of Representatives picked the president.

Two of the other **candidates**, John Quincy Adams and Henry Clay, made a deal. Clay was a leader in the House. Adams was picked as president. Adams then named Clay to an important government job. Andrew was angry. He was also determined to run again. Andrew and his supporters formed the beginnings of the Democratic Party.

In 1828, Andrew ran for president again. Adams and his supporters were mean. They said Andrew was dishonest, uneducated, and dangerous. They also spread gossip about Rachel. Andrew won the election. In December, Rachel had a heart attack and died. Andrew returned to Washington, D.C., without the woman he loved.

Andrew Jackson almost won the 1824 presidential election.

President Jackson

Andrew received strong support from the common people. He was their hero. After he was sworn in, many of Andrew's admirers came to the White House. During the party, they jumped on the chairs. They broke the dishes. Things got so wild that Andrew had to sneak out a window.

Andrew faced big problems while he was president. Some states did not want to obey federal laws. South Carolina said it did not have to obey a law. Andrew said it did. South Carolina said it would leave the United States. Andrew threatened to send military men on navy ships to enforce the law. South Carolina backed down. This issue of states' rights would lead to the Civil War in 1861.

Andrew wanted to get rid of the national bank. This bank held the government's money. The rich men who ran the bank did not like to lend money to common people. Andrew did not think that was fair. The common people had elected him. Congress passed a law that let the bank continue to operate. Andrew refused to sign the bill.

Andrew Jackson faced big problems while he was president.

Trail of Tears

In the early 1800s, many Americans wanted to move into Alabama, Mississippi, and Georgia. They wanted to farm. The land was perfect for growing cotton and grain. The land belonged to the Indians. They were known as the Five Civilized Tribes. They were the Cherokee, Chickasaw, Choctaw, Creek, and Seminole Indians. They were very successful farmers. Andrew asked them to sell their land. When the Indians refused he threatened them. Congress passed laws that forced the Indians to move.

The Indians had to move west of the Mississippi River. The area was called Indian Territory. It later became the state of Oklahoma. The Cherokee were forced to move there in 1838. They became hungry and sick along the way. Thousands of Cherokee died. This move west became known as the Trail of Tears.

Settlers got the land they wanted. But the Indians paid a very high price for their success.

Andrew Jackson threatened the Five Civilized Tribes after they refused to sell their land.

The Final Years

Andrew was elected president again in 1832. He decided not to run in 1836. Andrew was 70 years old when he left Washington in March 1837.

He returned to the Hermitage, but he was not a happy man. He missed Rachel. After she died, the house seemed empty. He also worried about money.

Andrew was not in very good health. The duels he had when he was young hurt his body. Doctors were not able to do much to help the old general. Andrew Jackson died on June 8, 1845.

Andrew Jackson went from a log cabin to the White House. He was a common man loved by the American people. He was a lawyer, a congressman, a war hero, a plantation owner, and a president.

Andrew helped the young United States expand and change. He was one of America's greatest presidents.

Andrew and Rachel Jackson are buried at the Hermitage.

Words from Andrew Jackson

"As long as our government is administered for the good of the people, and is regulated by their will … it will be worth defending."

From Jackson's inaugural address,
March 4, 1829

"There are no necessary evils in government. Its evils exist only in its abuses."

From Jackson's veto message to Congress,
July 10, 1832

Important Dates in Andrew Jackson's Life

1767—Born March 15 at Waxhaw settlement, South Carolina

1780-1781—Fights in Revolutionary War; captured and wounded by British

1794—Marries Rachel Donelson Robards

1796—Elected to House of Representatives; first congressman from Tennessee

1797-1798—Serves in U.S. Senate

1812-1815—Commands troops in battles against the Indians and British

1817-1818—Commands troops in battles against Seminole Indians

1823—Elected to U.S. Senate

1828—Elected president; Rachel Jackson dies

1832—Re-elected president

1837—Leaves Washington, D.C., for the Hermitage

1845—Dies and is buried at the Hermitage

Words to Know

candidate—person who seeks an office

colony—group of people who settle in a distant land but remain under control of their native country. The 13 British colonies in North America became the original United States.

descendant—offspring of a certain person or group

duel—formal fight between two people armed with deadly weapons

militia—citizens who are not professional soldiers called to serve in the armed services during emergencies

Read More

Meltzer, Milton. *Andrew Jackson and His America*. New York: Franklin Watts, 1993.

Osinski, Alice. *Andrew Jackson*. Chicago: Children's Press, 1987.

Quackenbush, Robert M. *Who Let Muddy Boots Into the White House?: A Story of Andrew Jackson*. New York: Prentice-Hall Books For Young Readers, 1986.

Sandler, Martin W. *Presidents: A Library of Congress Book*. New York: HarperCollins, 1995.

Useful Addresses and Internet Sites

The Ladies' Hermitage Association
4580 Rachel's Lane
The Hermitage
Nashville, TN 37076

Tennessee State Museum
505 Deaderick Street
Nashville, TN 37219

A Brief Biography of Andrew Jackson
http://www.panix.com/userdirs/hal/jksn-bio.htm
White House for Kids
http://www.whitehouse.gov/WH/kids/html/kidshome.html

Index